CW01669764

# THE LONDON BOROUGH OF HACKNEY IN OLD PHOTOGRAPHS

BEFORE 1914

THE SPIRE OF THE NEW ST MARY'S CHURCH, Stoke Newington, rises above the mists of the graveyard, at the turn of the century. Designed by Sir George Gilbert Scott, it was completed in 1858 and the spire added in 1890. Bomb-damaged in the Second World War it was fully restored in 1957. A view looking south-east.

# THE LONDON BOROUGH OF HACKNEY IN OLD PHOTOGRAPHS

BEFORE 1914

FROM HACKNEY ARCHIVES DEPARTMENT

COMPILED BY
DAVID MANDER

ALAN SUTTON
1989

Alan Sutton Publishing
Gloucester

First published 1989



**British Library Cataloguing in Publication Data**

Hackney in old photographs.
1. London. Hackney (London Borough), history
I. Mander, David
942.1'44

ISBN 0-86299-677-5

## DEDICATION

For Janice

Typesetting and origination by
Alan Sutton Publishing
Printed in Great Britain by
Dotesios Printers Limited

# CONTENTS

THE OLD TOWN HALL of 1802, with the old church tower behind it. The lamp in the foreground adjoined the old entrance to Hackney Station, by Bohemia Place; a new one opened on the other side of the road in December 1870. Biggs the funeral furnishers' premises were demolished in the 1880s to allow trams to enter the Bohemia Place depot. All the buildings south of the old town hall were completely destroyed on the night of 19/20 March 1941 by bombing.

# INTRODUCTION

The spread of the use of cameras coincided with an accelerated period of change for Hackney, in which the march of bricks and mortar covered the fields and streets still retaining buildings from the rural past were transformed to serve bustling suburbs. This book covers the time when many of those changes took place, from the late 1860s until just before the First World War. I hope it will take the reader back to scenes that have subsequently become almost unrecognizable through building and twentieth-century redevelopment in Hackney, Stoke Newington and Shoreditch.

Visual recording of the past has long antecedents in the area. The Tyssen family, at one time the largest local landowners, actively commissioned artists and architects from the late eighteenth century onwards to record local buildings that were under threat. At least one of the more enterprising ones, George Hawkins, turned his watercolours and sketches into commercial engravings for sale in local shops. Alive to a good business opportunity, some local stationers produced their own views and from the middle of the last century a few turned to the new art of photography. Some of this would have been studio portrait work, but one cameraman, George James, whose business was first in Church Street, Hackney (later part of Mare Street) and then in Clarence Road, took his cumbersome equipment out onto the streets.

James is the first identified local photographer whose work survives in any quantity. There was no quick process of turning photographs into postcards. Instead each print had to be individually made from the negative and pasted down on small mounts. James, working from the mid-1860s, stuck to small *carte-de-visite* sized prints, but a competitor, Alfred Braddock, working from the late 1870s to about 1910, used a size closer to the modern postcard, though he too printed up each card individually. Braddock seems to have had a strong loyalty to the Mare Street, Clapton, Homerton and River Lea areas, since even after moving to Hornsey in the 1890s he and his son returned over the next 20 years to record the changing scene. Braddock's work was supplemented by mass-produced postcards from the turn of the century: in some cases an enterprising photographer would take a view of a street and then sell the limited run of postcards to the occupiers.

The nostalgic approach to photography in the area may help to explain the relative strengths and weaknesses of what survives. By the era of commercial photography Shoreditch, Dalston, De Beauvoir Town and much of South Hackney were already built up. Contemporary attitudes to views of these areas in the later nineteenth century would be similar to ours now on the housing estates of the 1950s and 1960s and so we are dependent on family photographs – where these survive. Interiors are also rare, as the technical equipment was simply not up to the job. Only the affluent middle classes could afford a commission like the album of views of the Gaviller family home that features in the last chapter of this book.

The photographs I have selected are all taken from prints held in the visual and archives collections of Hackney Council's Archives Department. New material has been taken in from other institutions, notably the collections held by the Greater London Record Office and English Heritage. Appeals have also resulted in many family photographs being loaned for copying and the department is grateful to all those who have done so, as well as to those whose photographs appear here.

The earliest view in the book is from 1855; the latest from just after the First World War, showing a scene that would have been little changed from ten years earlier. I have not stuck rigidly to the present borough boundaries: some subjects are just outside the area or donated by local people. I have also used a selection of views from the Union Workhouse school at Brentwood where many Hackney and Shoreditch children would have been sent. Nor has area coverage been equal; this is in part imposed on me by the limitations of the collection. I have taken the opportunity of putting together much of George James' work on the Mare Street area, because this was unrecognized as such before and constitutes the earliest street survey in the collection.

This book was originally conceived as a work with fewer views to be published by Hackney Council. I am pleased that publication by Alan Sutton has enabled it to be expanded as more views have been included and research has enabled us to provide better dates for many photographs. In the process one item has had its date changed from *c.* 1900 to prior to 1865! I have also tried to describe where possible what happened to many prominent buildings. This is a book about Hackney's past, but in recording the built environment, the people who made it and lived in it should not be forgotten. Alfred Braddock was often careful to include passers-by in his compositions, realizing perhaps that static views were not so popular.

The book is arranged roughly in area order, starting at Mare Street and working round the borough to finish at Upper Clapton. The River Lea forms Hackney's eastern boundary and this has its own chapter. The last four sections look at leisure activities, poverty and sickness, education and the domestic scene. Regrettably space has not allowed the inclusion of a map, but in researching the book I worked with the excellent series of reprinted Ordnance survey maps produced by Alan Godfrey and it should be possible to track down the exact location of the majority of the views in this book from these. Many of the Hackney subjects also feature in the recollections of the area by Benjamin Clarke in his *Glimpses of Ancient Hackney and Stoke Newington* (1893, reprinted with a new introduction 1986) and this book in part forms a pictorial supplement to that work.

Owners of original photographs other than Hackney Council are thanked at the end of this work. I have drawn substantially on the work of George James and Alfred Braddock, and to a lesser extent on an album produced by John Carey, a Clapton man. Rather than repeat credits I have used the initials of these three after their photographs. Lastly, special thanks to two former members of Hackney Archives Department's staff: Jon Newman who worked on the first version of this book on picture selection, text writing and also researched Alfred Braddock, and Jenny Golden, who helped with picture research for the new edition. Writing in 1892 Benjamin Clarke urged an enterprising photographer to record a building before it vanished. We are lucky that many such records survive of the streets and the people who lived in them and I hope that this selection will provide a glimpse of a long gone Hackney.

David Mander, Borough Archivist
June 1989

SECTION ONE

# Mare Street (Narrow Way)

THE NORTH END OF THE NARROW WAY, MARE STREET, looking towards Ward's corner and the Prince of Wales public house at the end of Dalston Lane. The tram tracks are very new, for this route was not opened until July 1873 by the North Metropolitan Tramways and this photograph by George James may have been taken just after construction was completed in late 1872 or early 1873. As the shadows show, James was up early in the morning to achieve the uncluttered street scene. This and the next seven pages are all James' work and together are a portrait of the part of Mare Street that was called Church Street until 1868 – from the junction with Lower Clapton Road to the present town hall. They record a village street that was transformed in the ensuing 30 years into a bustling shopping thoroughfare. (GJ)

THE WEST SIDE OF MARE STREET, from the Three Cranes public house (No. 359) to No. 377. Nos. 371–3, just beyond the two low buildings, were Axtens the drapers, thought by the local historian Benjamin Clarke to have been the oldest such firm in Hackney. McDonalds and British Home Stores now occupy this site. According to Clarke the three Cranes began life as herons, from the arms of Sir Thomas Heron, Master of Henry VIII's Jewel House, who was partly responsible for rebuilding Hackney church around 1520. The Three Cranes was reputedly established for the workmen. Rebuilt by 1870 it ceased to be a pub before 1884. Summer 1873. (GJ)

THE SHOPS just to the north of the preceeding photograph (Nos. 373–9). Frederick Goodchild had just established his jewellery business, taking over from S. Burton. Summer 1873. (GJ)

THE CORNER OF MARE STREET AND AMHURST ROAD. Nos 341–5 Mare Street, the Eight Bells public house and the old town hall. The Railway public house now stands on the site of Winny's haberdashers shop, which had gone by 1884. Summer 1873. (GJ)

THE CORNER OF MARE STREET AND AMHURST ROAD looking towards the North London railway bridge, a little earlier than the above view. Mr Winny had yet to extend his shop. The four-wheeled 'growler' is waiting for hire, possibly by passengers from Hackney Station, still on the east side of the street. Tramway construction had not commenced, though the ornamentation on the wall would suggest that the drapers Matthew Rose had built their new shop-front on to Amhurst Road. *c.* 1870. (GJ)

MARE STREET, west side looking towards the railway bridge. The two shops next to the bridge are Green and Branscombe, a drapers business at Nos. 333–5 Mare Street, later taken over by Matthew Rose and now the site of Woolworths. Just to the south is the entrance to the vanished Brook Place which, with the three buildings to the south, was cleared for the construction of Graham Road in 1870, shortly after this view was taken. (GJ)

THE OPPOSITE SIDE OF THE STREET from No. 292, with the King's Head public house in the distance, and George James standing opposite the junction with Morning Lane. The policeman has a wary eye on the barrow and although the tram tracks are in place there are still no trams. A wet afternoon, *c.* 1873. (GJ)

A CLOSER VIEW OF THE EAST SIDE, this time from No. 280, Mrs Christmas the hatter, *c.* 1870. All the buildings on this side of the road have gone, the majority cleared for road widening. History does not record the quality or otherwise of Pash's boots. (GJ)

THE EAST SIDE AGAIN, from No. 322, Holtham the tailors. The man outside the King's Head appears to be selling potted plants. An afternoon *c.* 1870. (GJ)

THE KING'S HEAD AND CUSTOMERS, one late afternoon *c.* 1867. There is no record to tell us whether landlord, J. Whitehead, joined them (his name is just visible on the glass of the bracket light). The old King's Head dates back to at least the sixteenth century. The author of *Our Local Sketches* records that one landlord changed the name to Cromwell's Head in the Civil War, but was not quick enough to change it back in 1660 and was whipped and pilloried. The pub was demolished in 1879 and rebuilt; its successor was in turn demolished before 1905. (GJ)

THE EIGHT BELLS AND THE RAILWAY COAL OFFICES, looking south towards the North London railway bridge, with a signal just visible above the buildings. Street traders are out in force. *c.* 1869. (GJ)

THE IVY HOUSE and the pair of houses to the north, on the west side of Mare Street at the corner with Richmond Road. The Ivy House, built in the eighteenth century, was leased to Benjamin Smith. In 1838 he built the houses next door (later became Nos. 273–5 Mare Street). There were many large houses on the southern section of Mare Street, of which only the Landsdowne Club house remains. The Ivy House, taken over by the Salvation Army by 1894 as a maternity hospital, was demolished by 1926 to build a petrol station. Nos. 273–5 lasted longer, being used as a clothing factory until the late 1960s. (GJ)

HACKNEY CHURCHYARD, looking south-west towards the last of the row of old houses that backed on to Bohemia Place, named after associations with the Black and White House, which stood on the site until 1796. This had housed Elizabeth, sister of Charles I and wife of the hapless Elector of the Palatinate who fled from Prague after the battle of the White Mountain in 1618. Elizabeth, briefly Queen of Bohemia, was thereafter known as the Winter Queen. The churchyard was cleared in 1893; the houses fronting it survived until 19/20 March 1941, when they were bombed. (GJ)

HACKNEY'S SECOND TOWN HALL, opened in 1866 and seen here decorated for a special occasion, possibly the opening itself. Built to house the expanded local government needed for Hackney, after the 1855 Metropolis Management Act created the vestries, it was in turn demolished as inadequate in 1937; the site is now flower beds in front of the present town hall. *c.* 1866 or 1867. (GJ)

A VERY SPECIAL OUTING gathers outside the Crown public house, No. 418 Mare Street, *c.* 1898, with no less than three coaches and fours. Wherever they are going they are all well wrapped up!

A BUSY SCENE in 1904, looking north. There were still another five years of the horse tram service to go before the route was electrified in 1909. (AB)

THE JUNCTION WITH AMHURST ROAD AND THE NORTH LONDON RAILWAY, looking south in 1886. The signal box was built after the station moved to the west side of the road in 1870 and would appear to have either been damaged in the bombing of 1941, or shortly afterwards. Beyond the bridge substantial rebuilding has taken place since George James was active. (AB)

HACKNEY'S PREMIER DEPARTMENT STORE at the turn of the century was Matthew Rose & Sons. This is their Mare Street shop, Nos. 347–57, *c.* 1900. By this time the business had expanded into Nos. 2–18 Amhurst Road. The Mare Street premises had opened in 1868, when Rose's expanded from their original shop of *c.* 1852, at No 353 Mare Street. Rose's closed down in 1936 and their premises were later taken over by Marks and Spencers.

HACKNEY STATION and junction with Amhurst Road, posters to the fore. Postcard, c. 1905.

HACKNEY CHURCHYARD looking west towards the old church tower and the Rowe Chapel, winter 1886, before the clearance of 1892. The Rowe Chapel was a family tomb rather than a place of worship, built by Sir Henry Rowe in 1614. It was in poor condition when in 1877 an unfortunate sextoness was killed while conducting a tour. Later repaired, its condition again deteriorated and it had been demolished by 1913. (AB)

MARE STREET, from the Cock public house looking north towards the railway bridge, with W.G. Fish's pawnbroker's sign very much in evidence. Compare with the photograph on p. 12; in seventeen years much of this side of Mare Street had been rebuilt. 1887. (AB)

THE OTHER SIDE OF THE STREET, also 1887, showing the rebuilt King's Head public house and rather more bustle than in the earlier photographs of George James. (AB)

MARE STREET looking south and showing Nos. 305 to 279, the Britannia public house. Beyond the pub the row of trees mark the site of the town hall. The entrance to the Ship public house can just be seen, and the three low houses next to the Britannia were later to be demolished to build the Hackney Empire. An early summer morning in 1884. (AB)

FULL CEREMONIAL for the opening of Hackney Central Library in 1908. The Prince and Princess of Wales attended, along with a division of the Household Cavalry, seen here passing the Britannia public house and the Hackney Empire, 28 May 1908.

THE HACKNEY EMPIRE and a busy Mare Street *c.* 1905. The Empire had opened in 1901, designed by Frank Matcham and seating 3,000 people. It was part of Oswald Stoll's holdings until his death in 1942 and many famous stars, including Marie Lloyd, played there. After a period as a bingo hall it has now reopened as a very lively theatre again, the domes and statue of the lady have been restored.

SECTION TWO

# Mare Street (south of the Town Hall)

THE NAME MARE STREET is derived from the Middle English Meare, meaning a boundary and referring to the original settlement which was down by the boundary with Bethnal Green at the bottom of the street. Thus the name has nothing to do with horses, though many passed this way, providing a good business for smiths. This photograph shows Child's forge when it was being run by T. Corby, the local vet, who also used No. 263 Mare Street. James Child had founded the business some time before 1847 and the name was obviously worth retaining. The forge and the adjacent building's site was cleared to build Hackney Central Library. *c.* 1890.

NOS. 209 TO 213 MARE STREET, part of the group of houses north of Fortescue Avenue, almost opposite the Catholic Apostolic Church, *c.* 1902. Miss Elizabeth Newman had kept the servants' agency for many years, a reminder of the great demand for domestic servants in many Hackney houses at this time. It is to be hoped that John Sturch did not get his meat too dusty! This little group of houses were cleared away before 1913.

NOS. 224–8 MARE STREET, east side, at the corner with Darnley Road, *c.* 1905. This terrace was originally named after the builder, Spackman. The larger bow-fronted house on the end lost part of its garden and was altered when Darnley Road was cut through in the early 1860s. For many years it had been home to various doctors, one of whom was the local historian Benjamin Clarke, who lived there from 1850 to 1863. The terrace still stands.

A LITTLE FURTHER TO THE SOUTH was another large terrace on the corner with Devonshire Road (now Brenthouse Road), also *c.* 1905. By the turn of the century many of the large houses on Mare Street had become unfashionable for private residents and had been put to institutional or business use. The house on the corner was used as a laundry.

MARE STREET BAPTIST CHURCH, which stood on the west side, just south of the junction with Helmsley Street. Built by a congregation that had its origins in Shore Place (now Shore Road) in 1798, the church moved to Mare Street shortly after 1811. The first building on the site burnt down in 1854 and this splendid building replaced it. The new church was badly damaged by bombs in 1940 and again in 1945, then demolished. The congregation now meets in Frampton Park Baptist Church. Photograph taken during the ministry of J. Haslam Jones, 1901–11. (AB)

MARE STREET east side from about level with the junction with Pemberton Place, looking north. The building on the corner is Lady Holles girls' school; the building with the protruding shop-front, used as dining rooms, was once a chemist's shop, and was the birthplace of Benjamin Clarke. The buildings south of the school had all been demolished by 1905 and the site and the school now form part of Cordwainers College. *c.* 1900.

MARE STREET, east side from No. 106 with Freeman's the builders, looking south, showing the Church of St John the Baptist and the spire of Cambridge Heath Congregational Church in the distance. The buildings to the right are the south part of the Triangle. Cambridge Heath Congregational Church was demolished shortly after 1936 and the site incorporated into St Joseph's Hospice. St John's Catholic Church was rebuilt after the Second World War; every other building in this view has also disappeared. *c.* 1873. (GJ)

MARE STREET, Nos. 92 to 106, looking north. Builders' yards feature prominently in this view, taken almost 30 years after the one above. Tantalilizingly the shop on the corner has escaped listing in local directories. From its opening hours (from 5 a.m.!) it would seem to cater for the very early shopper. *c.* 1900.

ST THOMAS SQUARE CONGREGATIONAL CHURCH was built by an Independent congregation in 1772. In the top view of 1886 it was still a church, but it changed hands in 1896 when the Presbyterians took over. By 1914 it had changed hands again and the lower view shows the building in its new guise as a cinema. It was later substantially rebuilt and is now a bingo hall.

THE TRIANGLE, MARE STREET, looking north *c.* 1912. Postcard by J. Kingston & Co. Only the Warburton Arms (see just behind the electric tramcar) of the buildings in this view survives.

W.J. BUSH'S DESPATCH VEHICLES outside their Ash Grove factory *c.* 1914. Bush's who made chemicals and flavouring essences, moved to the Hackney site from Bishopsgate in 1885. The company later became part of the Bush Boake Allen group and moved from Ash Grove in 1974. The site is now a London Transport bus garage.

THE SOUTH SIDE OF THE TRIANGLE and the corner of Westgate Street c. 1910. The row to the south was shortly to be demolished but the fine Georgian houses (Nos. 107–9) survived until July 1944 when they were bombed. André's music school had closed about 14 years before.

HACKNEY RECTORY, seen from the lawns *c.* 1890. This had been built in 1705, after complaints from the then vicar, Peter Newcome, that the old vicarage on Church Street was 'in a ruinous condition, no windows left . . . the stairs decayed, the floors broken and the timber, a great part of it rotten.' Newcome also complained about the noise and dirt from the street. After an inspection from fellow clergymen (including the antiquarian John Strype) Newcome got his way and the old vicarage, which stood to the north of the old town hall, was demolished. The site was used to widen the road and extend the churchyard. Newcome's vicarage, later the rectory, was substantially rebuilt by Archdeacon John James Watson between 1826 and 1832, giving it the appearance seen in this view. In turn it was replaced by a new rectory on a different alignment in the 1950s. Christopher Urswick's house or Church House, was only in use as a rectory by Urswick, who died in 1522. After that date it was used as a parochial school and for vestry meetings until it was demolished in 1802 and replaced by the old town hall.

THIS HOUSE which stood on Lower Clapton Road, on the west side just south of Clapton Passage, was leased by Dr Joseph Priestley from 1792–4. During his residence he preached at the Gravel Pit Chapel. The house was used as a school in the 1870s and was demolished c. 1883.

TAKEN IN THE SUMMER of 1882, this view shows the north side of Clapton Passage under construction; Priestley's house is in the background on the right. Plastering is still under way and the builders have paused for the photographer. The applicant for building permission was Christopher Ruthven, who may be the frock-coated man with the wooden leg. (AB)

SECTION THREE

# Lower Clapton and Lea Bridge

LOWER CLAPTON used to be that area of the high road between St John's Church and the junction with Lea Bridge Road. In the early nineteenth century it consisted of large houses and a few shops, with only one major development, Clapton Square, in the south. But rapid development from the middle of the century covered the fields and many of the larger houses, some of which were captured by photographers just before their demise, were demolished. Now it is hard to define where Lower Clapton stops and Homerton begins. This view of Lower Clapton Road looking east from opposite the present police station was taken one summer *c.* 1909 and shows the King's Hall and Hackney public baths, built in 1896.

THE NORTH-EAST AND EAST SIDES OF CLAPTON SQUARE, in 1892 and 1908 respectively. The square was laid out in 1816, though one house in the north-east corner dated from the previous century. Voss' house and the one to the south of Clapton Passage were demolished to build Cavendish and St John's mansions respectively in 1899–1901. The lower view shows parts of both blocks and the houses on the west side which were destroyed in the Blitz in November 1940. (AB)

THE EAST SIDE OF CLAPTON SQUARE, *c.* 1905.

THE CORNER OF LOWER CLAPTON AND URSWICK ROADS in 1884, showing the 'For Sale' signs up in front of the last of the pair of houses forming part of 'Five Houses'. These were built on land taken from the former Hackney House estate, after the latter was demolished *c.* 1800. The name 'Five Houses' originally applied to all the houses, but by the 1880s all except two had been demolished and the one viewed here had taken the name to itself. Lesbia Road was built on the site; in turn this has now been replaced by a health centre. (For the other house see p. 36.) (AB)

GIFFEN'S THE SADLER'S SHOP, probably taken in the spring of 1873. This tiny pair of weather-boarded houses stood on the west side of Lower Clapton Road on a site just to the north of the White Hart. By 1882 this and the neighbouring houses had been replaced by a terrace called Donegal Place and Ebenezer Giffen had moved into No. 2. (GJ)

DRAYTON HOUSE, LOWER CLAPTON ROAD. The neighbour of 'Five Houses' (p. 35) and not, as labelled by the photographer, Portland Place. Comparing this with 'Five Houses' one can see that they were built as a pair, with stable blocks backing on to each other, a corner of which can be seen on the left. The last occupants were C.E. Hilton's firm of estate agents. *c.* 1883 (AB)

ARGENT'S CONFECTIONERY SHOP AND POST OFFICE, Lower Clapton Road, west side, opposite the junction with Linscott Road. John Argent seems to have been a bird fancier in his spare time judging by the cage by the window. Behind the shop are two private houses. Summertime, *c.* 1868.

A LITTLE FURTHER UP THE ROAD looking back towards the shop in the view above the Windsor Castle public house. The building in the foreground, which still stands, was then the Clapton Registry Office. Summer 1894. (AB)

TAKEN TEN YEARS BEFORE THE LAST PHOTOGRAPH, this view shows the Windsor Castle and the buildings to the south on the corner of Goulton Road, George Pratt the tailor, and Charles Witherden, butcher. Pratt's shop had been unchanged since the early years of the nineteenth century and both shops lasted until October 1940 when they were damaged by bombing and later demolished. The lower view shows the Windsor Castle and customers *c.* 1883. The pub was rebuilt early in the 1890s. (AB)

CROMWELL HOUSE LODGE AND DURHAM HOUSE *c.* 1884. Cromwell House Lodge was probably a seventeenth century building that had been given a new frontage and altered in the early nineteenth century; both houses were in use as private schools in the nineteenth century. Cromwell Lodge was demolished shortly after this view was taken for the construction of Atherden Road, but Durham House survived, converted into shops until at least the late 1930s. (AB)

CLAPTON POND from the junction with Millfields Road. Winter 1882.

THE LOCAL POSTMAN AND FRIENDS gathered at the south end of Clapton Pond, summer 1885. As the sign makes clear, the pond was private property, owned by the Powell family. It was drained in 1893, but strong local protests galvanized the local authority into action, and the refilled pond was purchased by Hackney Vestry in 1895. (AB)

CLAPTON POND looking west towards Sion House and the terrace divided into Byland House (this end) and the Gaviller family house (see p. 158–9). Sion House, which may have been named by an earlier Jewish owner, was owned by the Berger family, whose factory was at nearby Homerton, at the time of this 1880 view. It was later used by successive doctors and was demolished in March 1933. (AB)

POND HOUSE AND PART OF ST JAMES' TERRACE seen from the west side of Clapton Pond *c.* 1890. Pond House and the adjoining houses of the terrace still stand, but the houses further south were demolished to build Mildenhall Road in 1890. The end house (below), Bow House, survived until 1930 when it was also destroyed along with its neighbour apparently to build the public lavatory now on the site. (AB)

FROM LEFT TO RIGHT this view shows Lime Tree and White Cottages, Miss Rutt's house and the Bishop Wood Almshouses, in 1884. The small houses, known as Clarke's Cottages, and Miss Rutt's house were demolished *c.* 1890, when Newick Road and the terrace originally called St James' Villas were built. (AB)

POND LANE PATH ran from the junction between Rushmore and Mayola Roads north-west towards Pond Lane (now Millfields Road) on the present alignment of the rest of Rushmore Road. To the right is Pond Lane Nursery, which survived in truncated form until the early years of the twentieth century, though much of its grounds were soon to be taken by builders. This reminder of how rural parts of Hackney looked a century ago is from 1888. (AB)

THIS MUCH PHOTOGRAPHED GROUP of weather-boarded cottages stood on the north side of Millfields Road near the junction with Clapton Pond and just east of Bow House (p. 41). Recognized as being under threat from the late 1880s they were swept away in 1896. A view of 1886. (AB)

ONCE THE TRAVELLER in the last century was clear of Pond Farm, Pond Lane became a muddy farm track leading to a small footbridge over the Hackney Cut. Braddock captured it on film before the builders moved in. His photograph is taken looking west from somewhere near what was later the junction with Chatsworth Road in 1879. (AB)

BISHOP WOOD'S ALMSHOUSES, a view looking north-east after St James' Villas had been built, taken *c*. 1900. Originally endowed by Dr Thomas Wood, Bishop of Lichfield and Coventry, in his will of 1690 for ten poor Hackney widows, the almshouses also include a small chapel, restored in 1845, and said to be the smallest church in England. Later renovation work included alterations to the chapel window, but the almshouses are still in use today. (AB)

THE WOOD FAMILY were early owners of Clapton House, which stood on the east side of Lower Clapton Road, on the site of Thistlethwaite Road. The seventeenth-century house passed to the Powell family, who owned much property in Clapton, including Clapton Pond. They in turn leased it out and it was often in use as a private school before being demolished *c*. 1885. It is seen here empty in 1884.

THE WHITE HART, Lower Clapton Road, early summer 1890. This building replaced an earlier public house which burnt down in the early 1830s and was in turn replaced by the present one in the early 1890s. (AB)

CRICKETFIELD ROAD looking towards the junction with Downs Road, in the spring of 1890. Behind the cart can be seen the Clapton Wesleyan Sunday school, built in 1880. The Wesleyan church stood on Lower Clapton Road but was abandoned after bomb damage in the Second World War, when the congregation moved into the Sunday school, which is still the local Methodist church. (AB)

THE JUNCTION of Upper and Lower Clapton roads with Lea Bridge Road, looking down Lea Bridge Road in 1892. The fountain in the centre of the road was moved in 1908 to the junction of Amhurst and Rectory Roads, but the statuette has now vanished. All the buildings in this view were cleared for the construction of the present Lea Bridge roundabout in the early 1970s. (AB)

G.H. KEEN'S DAIRY AND GROCERY SHOP, No. 124 Clarence Road, *c*. 1905, with the delivery trolley to the fore. This would have gone round from house to house with fresh milk.

THE TURNPIKE TOLL-GATE on Lea Bridge Road in 1870, built in 1757. The gothic windows were added in alterations of 1818. Lea Bridge Road remained a turnpike road with its own trustees until July 1872 and map evidence would suggest that the toll house, which stood at the junction with Middlesex Wharf, just before the bridge, was demolished shortly afterwards. (GJ)

THE FIRST TWO YEARS of the present century were abnormally dry and drought was a serious problem. But the weather made up for this in June 1903 when a 60-hour rainstorm beginning on Saturday 13 June left the Lea Valley impassable for a day or so. By the following Tuesday the waters had subsided a little and tram horses were able to get through, as the photograph shows. The floods were so serious that Hackney Council organized a distress fund.

MR HUSON COPPIN'S SPLENDID SHOP, No. 41 Chatsworth Road, seen here in 1913. The proprietor also made artificial teeth, the mainstay of dentistry in an era in which most visits to the dentist ended in extractions. The different prices are for the materials used – the customer had a choice ranging from porcelain to gold.

WILLIAM HAMMER'S BUTCHERS SHOP, No. 93 Rendlesham Road (on the corner with Maury Road), c. 1910, with one of his regular customers in a Bath chair just about to be served. Hammer later joined Hackney Council and was Mayor from 1923–4.

NORTHWALD ROAD, north side Nos. 229–49 in July 1896. A view by John Carey, who lived in Ickburgh Road and was active photographing and collecting local views from 1880 to 1905. (JC)

CHATHAM PLACE STEAM LAUNDRY and the Woodhurst family, seen here *c.* 1900. The business, at No. 56, had gone by 1907.

SECTION FOUR

# Homerton

HOMERTON was one of the main areas of settlement within the parish of Hackney, and with land on the south side sloping gently down to Hackney Brook and the meadows and views over to the Lea to the north and east, it was an area of large houses. What changed the area was the construction of the North London Railway and estate development which packed in small houses, so that by the end of the last century it was one of the poorer areas in Hackney. Even so, Urswick Road, formerly Upper Homerton, still retained large houses, the last of which, Sutton House, can be seen in this view *c.* 1900. Sutton House dated from *c.* 1525 and was built on an H plan. Later altered, the house was divided in 1740 and the east wing rendered *c.* 1870. By the time of this view it was in use as the St John's Institute which provided accommodation and social activities for young men of Hackney. Bought by the National Trust in 1938, it stood empty after 1982, though recent activity by the newly-formed Sutton House Society has opened the house to the public again. As Hackney's oldest surviving domestic building, Sutton House forms a good introduction to Homerton.

ADJOINING SUTTON HOUSE is Sutton Place, one of Hackney's earliest terrace developments, built *c.* 1810 by a member of the Collins family (who also built the Paragon). This view of the south side is taken level with No. 5, then the offices of the Charity Organisation Society, *c.* 1900. (AB)

URSWICK ROAD looking south towards Sutton House, winter 1884. The first house on the left is Upton House, then in use as a truant school. This was the oldest house in Upper Homerton dating from the late seventeenth century. In 1704 it was bought by Richard Ryder, father of Dudley Ryder (later Attorney General). It was in this house – rather than the Black and White House, which the family moved to in 1723 – that Ryder wrote his diary. Upton House was demolished *c.* 1885 to be replaced with a purpose-built school. (AB)

NEXT DOOR TO UPTON HOUSE was Miss Rivaz's house, seen in the top view in 1886. Both views are by Braddock, the back view probably undertaken as a private commission. The house dated from the early eighteenth century and would appear to have been rebuilt in 1776–7. It remained in the possession of the Ryder family until 1785, when it was bought by David Powell. In turn the Powell family sold it to Charles Rivaz of Lloyds in 1847. The house acquired the gardens of its neighbour, which had been demolished by 1808. It had gone itself by 1905 and the site was incorporated in the school next door. (AB)

HOMERTON ROW looking south-east, showing part of the terrace that gave the street its old name of Alderman's Row, supposedly after the City worthies who lived there. This fine early eighteenth-century group was in the course of demolition at the time of this view to build Halidon Street, the southern portion of which has in turn been cleared. Summer 1887. (AB)

THIS LITTLE ROW OF COTTAGES stood on the south side of the road almost opposite the houses seen above. Beyond Eagle Terrace and its occupants can be seen Homerton Row Baptist Chapel and the Homerton Board School. (AB)

ST BARNABAS' CHURCH, HOMERTON was consecrated in 1847 and the tower added in 1852 by the local architect Arthur Ashipital. This crowded scene was taken in August 1911 during a railway strike, when soldiers were stationed on the tower and signalled to others on Hackney Marshes.

THE NORTHERN CORNER OF HOMERTON HIGH STREET showing Eagle House and the little row of shops, beyond which is the Peacock public house. Eagle House was used by George Glover, a dyer, at this date. Later it became a lodging house and was demolished in the early 1950s. Summer 1884. (AB)

NOS. 29–33 HOMERTON HIGH STREET, 1886. It was less common for a photographer to be able to get round the back of a building, but this has happened here. This range of timber-framed buildings attracted a great deal of attention in the 1880s and 1890s when they were first threatened with destruction. The historian Benjamin Clarke believed them to be a medieval residence of the Bishops of London, whose estates included this area; certainly the range was late medieval and its gradual destruction has deprived Hackney of a notable building. Demolition began at the east end and these and the two following photographs trace the last stages. Clarke urged 'some enterprising photographer [to] turn his camera on the Plough Public House [at the west end], take a careful view of its front in High Street' and hoped that a proper reconstruction would be made in due course. At least the photographer recorded the house, and, in including the backs, some indication of the state of poor repair the range had sunk into.

L O T XII.

A Freehold Eſtate, very eligibly ſituate at Homerton, a ſmall Diſtance from the preceding Lots; compriſing the old accuſtomed Public-Houſe, known by the Plough, with a Shuffleboard-Room, Stabling for ſix Horſes, Skittle-Ground, Store-Cellars, and Garden; late in the Poſſeſſion of Mrs. Harris, deceaſed, now her Executors, at a Ground-Rent of only 10l. per Annum: Suppoſed yearly Value 31 10 0

£700 Deacon

PART OF A SALE CATALOGUE of 1785 when the Ryder family sold the Plough public house. (H.A.D. LHB/CA 2/18)

THESE TWO VIEWS of the Plough and the adjacent row complete the story. The top one shows the whole range a year or so earlier. Timber baulks have been used to shore up part of the row. By 1887 all except the Plough had gone, and this was shortly afterwards to be completely rebuilt. This lower view, looking west, also shows Humberstones the pawnbrokers and Ram's Episcopal Chapel. (AB)

RAM'S EPISCOPAL CHAPEL was established by Stephan Ram in his garden in 1723 after a disagreement with the parish church. It became a chapel of ease and after 1775 had its own trustees and low church worship. In the 1890s one minister's daughter was less than taken with 'the long dingy building, capped by a little tower looking like a magnified pepper pot, looking just like a brewery'. Substantially repaired in the early 1920s, Rams closed in 1932 and the building went shortly after 1935. This view is from 1884. (AB)

HOMERTON COLLEGE'S SECOND BUILDING, No. 75 Homerton High Street, winter 1886. Congregationalists acquired an old house on the High Street in 1768 as a theological college and rebuilt it in 1824; this is the building seen here. After the later Homerton College was moved to Cambridge in 1892–3, the vacant building was taken over by the London School Board as a school for the deaf; it was demolished just after 1930. (AB)

HOMERTON HIGH STREET, *c.* 1890. A view looking east from Isabella Road towards the Peacock public house (see p. 55). Braddock has enlivened his view with a little group of people. Men in uniform were an especial favourite and every policeman in Hackney must have been pressed into service at some time. (AB)

SIDNEY ROAD looking west from Wick Road and including the Tiger public house. The Catholic church, opened in October 1877, was badly damaged by bombs in March 1941 and later rebuilt. Sidney Road had its name changed to Kenworthy Road in 1938. View of *c.* 1905.

THE OLD GRAVEL PIT CHAPEL, Chatham Place in 1884. The founding congregation had its origins in the Presbyterian meeting house opposite St Thomas Square. Divisions within the congregation caused the move to a site in Gravel Pit Field at the north end of Chatham Place in 1715. Considering the old Gravel Pit Chapel unsafe, the Unitarian congregation moved to a site further south down Chatham Place in 1809 and congregationalists moved in from 1811 to 1871, when they in turn moved to the present Round Chapel. After a period as a mission, the chapel was converted for industrial use and much transformed, though it still stands today, with a plaque commemorating the preaching of Joseph Priestley in 1792–3. (AB)

HACKNEY FREE AND PAROCHIAL SCHOOL and the New Gravel Pit Chapel, Chatham Place in 1886. The school was opened in 1811, when the old premises in Urswick's House in front of the town hall were abandoned, and remained in use until replaced by a school in Isabella Road in 1895. The building survived in industrial use until 1973. The New Gravel Pit Chapel of 1853 was less fortunate than its predecessor, having replaced a building of 1808, it was demolished in order to build flats in 1970. (AB)

IN THE 1880s MARSH HILL was a very quiet end of the parish, with the lane leading down to the marshes, mainly used by cattle going down to graze. The top view shows the group of houses facing on to what is now Kenworthy Road: beyond to the left is Marsh Lane. The second view is a close up of the rather Dutch-looking house in the the top view and beyond the Marshgate toll house. These houses would have been demolished *c.* 1897 to build Mabley and Chevet Streets. (AB)

THE MARSHGATE TOLL HOUSE, Marsh Hill, 1897. The road across the marshes had been subjected to a toll which was abolished in 1862, but the buildings remained in use as a farm until 1901, when they were also cleared for the completion of Mabley Street. They were opposite the junction with Adley Road.

BERGER'S PAINT FACTORY, Morning Lane, 1906. Lewis Berger had moved from Shadwell to a green field site with well and running water (the Hackney Brook) in 1780. The site, bounded by Morning Lane, Shepherds Lane and the North London Railway (after 1850) was gradually built up. Bergers finally moved in 1960 and now only the laboratory block of 1934 remains, in use as Hackney Council's Social Services building.

TWO MORE VIEWS OF THE FACTORY, both from the archives of the company, deposited with Hackney Archives Department. The top view of 1865 is taken from near the corner with Shepherds Lane and the present Berger Road. Behind is the lawn of the original family house, to the left the warehouse built above Hackney Brook, in front the reservoir created after the brook was culverted, and in the middle the works clock tower, built in the early nineteenth century and included in later rebuildings. The family moved from the factory site to large houses just to the north (Five Houses and the Priory) but the lawns and water remained until late into the 1890s. The lower view shows a group of workers by the loading bay in 1870. Berger employees were noted for their long periods of employment with the company.

SECTION FIVE

# South Hackney and Hackney Wick

RATHER THAN TAKE THE ECCLESIASTICAL BOUNDARIES of the parish of South Hackney, created in 1825 and later divided, I have not strayed west of Mare Street or north of Well Street. Much of this area of Hackney was developed rapidly after 1860, though there were earlier developments and much later infilling. Hackney Wick became the principal industrial area of Hackney and there are few early photographs. The introductory view is taken on the corner of Well Street and Mare Street, looking east. In the distance is Denmark Place (later Nos. 22–40 Well Street), one house of which was home to the local doctor and antiquarian John Thomas. The little space before the bakers leads into a tiny coach yard. Taken late one summer afternoon, probably in 1869. (GJ)

ST JOHN OF JERUSALEM, South Hackney, *c.* 1885. Steeplejacks are at work repairing the original spire of 1848, whose Kentish ragstone had been eaten into by 40 years of air pollution. The repaired spire was damaged in the Blitz and replaced after 1945. St John's was the second South Hackney church, replacing an earlier chapel that had stood on the north side of Well Street by St Thomas Place and was intended by its founder, Revd Henry Handley Norris, to dominate the neighbourhood.

TYPICAL OF THE SMALL SHOPS OF THE AREA was J.R. Ashby's bakers shop at No. 127 Well Street, believed by Benjamin Clarke to be the oldest bakery in Hackney. In the 1850s Ashby, seen here with his staff *c.* 1865, had also doubled up as the local post office. Behind the shop are the gables of older buildings on the site of the former Priory House of the Knights of St John. (GJ?)

PORTER'S FURNISHING SHOP, on the corner of Well Street and Havelock Road, *c.* 1902. This had been Frampton House, built in 1696, and survived until the post-war redevelopment. Behind it, built in the back garden, is the Bruce Hall Mission, run by Methodists largely for young people and demolished shortly after 1948.

WELL STREET was the principal shopping street of South Hackney. These two views, both *c.* 1905, show (top) the street from the junction with Cressett Street, looking north-east towards the chimneys of Berger's paint factory, and a view looking east from Balcorne Street to Holcroft Road (bottom). All the houses in the lower view on the north side and most on the south have now gone and this part of Well Street has lost the sense of being a busy narrow shopping area.

THE FORMER HACKNEY TERRACE, later Nos. 20–54 Cassland Road, seen here in 1910 with the horse tram about to make its return journey to West India Dock Road. Hackney Terrace was built in 1792 by Thomas Gigney on Cass Estate land and, in addition to individual gardens, each house had access to a communal private lawn, later built over when Meynall Crescent was built in 1894–5.

KING EDWARD ROAD, south side, from the junction with Shore Road, looking east. South Hackney was very much a prosperous middle-class suburb in the Edwardian period. These houses were all cleared to construct the Kingshold Estate in the late 1960s.

A CLOSER LOOK at one of the Hackney Terrace houses. This is No. 42 Cassland Road and a back view showing the garden and the bow windows that the majority of the terrace was built with. The children are members of the King family, who moved into the house *c.* 1911. The houses had lost their private lawns but still retained their long gardens, as they do today.

LAURISTON ROAD looking south *c.* 1904, with the horse tram and delivery cart very much in evidence. This part of Lauriston Road, known as the Broadway, had been a shopping centre from the 1860s, when the road was still Grove Street, but it was always eclipsed by the nearby Well Street market. A Charles Martin postcard.

SPELDHURST ROAD looking south to the junction with Southborough Road *c.* 1905 and typical of the streets on the Norris Estate, built after 1860 by Henry Bagge and Robert Morley, with streets named after Norris property in Kent and elsewhere. The west side of the road was demolished to build the Kingshold Estate.

A CLOSER LOOK at No. 12 Speldhurst Road with children who may have been members of the Andrews family, who lived in the house in 1905 about the time of this photograph. The view clearly shows details of the ironwork, the majority of which went for salvage in the Second World War. Perhaps local inhabitants will be inspired to do some restoration!

THE ROYAL HOTEL, Lauriston Road, *c.* 1900. Standing at the edge of Victoria Park, the Royal was always a popular stopping place for thirsty park-goers. The cast-iron urinal went before 1939, but ice cream sellers remain. Postcard by Albert Day.

VICTORIA PARK STATION, Cadogan Terrace, *c.* 1905. The North London Railway between Dalston and Bow opened in 1851 and the first Victoria Park and Hackney Wick station was built behind the White Lion on Wick Road. The Cadogan Terrace station opened in 1866 with platforms on the NLR and the Great Eastern line to Stratford. This in turn closed to passengers in 1943 and was demolished in 1970. The new Hackney Wick station is on a new site on the GER line. The old station site is now under the motorway; the last vestige is Station Gate in Victoria Park.

## SECTION SIX

# Dalston, Kingsland and London Fields

AT THE TURN OF THE NINETEENTH CENTURY Dalston and Kingsland were ribbon settlements confined to Kingsland Road and High Street and to Dalston Lane. Development began in the late 1820s and by the 1870s was almost complete, changing the former village streets into busy shopping areas. This first view *c.* 1905 is taken at the junction of Dalston Lane and Kingsland High Street looking north. On the east side shops include branches of Sainsburys and Boots, while the horse tram is bound for Stamford Hill. Most of the shops in this view still survive though heavy car and lorry traffic has replaced the almost empty roadway.

DALSTON LANE from the junction with Kingsland High Street, with the Crown and Castle public house on the right. The cluster of buses in the distance are stopping for Dalston Junction station. A view from just after the First World War.

DALSTON LANE, around 1905 looking west showing the old and new police stations to the right.

RITSON ROAD from Dalston Lane, looking towards the German Hospital, *c.* 1905. The spire belongs to the Hamburg Lutheran church, built to serve Hackney's large German community which left its previous site near Mansion House when the underground station was built on it in 1871. Altar rails by Grindling Gibbons were also moved to the new church.

DALSTON LANE and the junction with Graham Road in 1877. The iron church just visible through the trees on the left is the precursor of St Bartholomew's Church, bombed in the Second World War and now demolished except for part of the vicarage. A delivery man has paused on his rounds to the large houses in the centre, now used by the Red Cross and the local Labour Party.

KINGSLAND ROAD looking north, with the fire station and the Metropolitan Hospital on the left, again *c.* 1905. The fire station of about 1897 has now been replaced by a modern building.

THE EAST SIDE OF KINGSLAND ROAD, from about No. 16, looking north, *c.* 1910.

STOKE NEWINGTON SYNAGOGUE, Shacklewell Lane, 1905. The original Jewish immigrants to the East End in the nineteenth century, gradually moved northwards to Hackney and Stoke Newington and built themselves places of worship, including this one, which opened in 1902. It is now used as a mosque.

ST MICHAEL AND ALL ANGELS CHURCH, vicarage and schools, seen in the late 1870s. The parish of St Michael was taken out of South Hackney and the church consecrated in 1864. The schools were opened in 1872 and the vicarage built in 1873. The tower was a later addition. The church suffered bomb damage in February 1945 in the same raid that finished off Mare Street Baptist Church, and the ruin was cleared away in 1956.

PONWALL ROAD CONGREGATIONAL CHURCH, on the corner with Norwich Road, was one of many back-street Nonconformist churches in the area, in this case serving that area of Shoreditch just to the north of Regent's Canal. Built in 1864 it was part of the area designated for redevelopment by Shoreditch Council and demolished *c.* 1950. This view dates from the turn of the century.

STOKE NEWINGTON ROAD looking north from the junction with Walford Road, showing West Hackney Church, consecrated in 1824 when the old parish of Hackney was divided into three. It was badly damaged by bombs in September 1940 and replaced by a modern building. The tram service from Stamford Hill was electrified in September 1909.

TWO VIEWS OF BROADWAY MARKET *c.* 1911, the top one looking south from the junction with Westgate Street, with the Cat and Mutton public house on the left, and the lower looking north from Ada Street towards the Lord Duncan. Both views show what a lively shopping street the market had become by Edwardian times, from its small beginnings as a row of shops called Duncans Place, built at the north end in the late 1820s. Renamed the Broadway in 1881, the present name was adopted in 1937.

'THE HACKNEY AND KINGSLAND GAZETTE' OFFICES, No. 440 Kingsland Road, *c.* 1905. The *Gazette*, launched in 1864, was originally a vehicle for the local Reform party, but these honorary contributors were replaced by the printer, Charles Potter, who substituted a paid editor and staff. The paper moved to its present site in 1958 and the Potter family remained in control until 1988.

SECTION SEVEN

# Shoreditch

SHOREDITCH was the first part of the present London Borough of Hackney to be completely built up. In the early eighteenth century development was clustered in the south around the High Street, with houses fronting Old Street and Kingsland Road, with settlement lines running up what became Hoxton Street and along the slightly later Hackney Road. Rapid development in the early nineteenth century produced a population peak of 129,000 in 1861; thereafter rehousing reduced the figure to 82,000 by 1939. Before 1914 the north retained its residential character, with trade, industry and shopping being concentrated further south. The photograph collection at Hackney has fewer pre-1914 Shoreditch views than for other areas of the borough, but the following pages should give an impression of the main streets, beginning with this view of the tower of St Leonard's Church, looking north-east to Hackney Road. A postcard by J. Cook & Sons c. 1900.

A VERY BUSY SCENE round St Leonard's Church *c.* 1905. Two- and four-wheeled cabs are waiting for business and a tram is about to edge its way into Hackney Road at the bottom left. The church dates from 1740 and was designed by George Dance the Elder. The full peal of twelve bells ('when we are rich . . .') were not heard for much of the nineteenth century, but were rehung shortly after the date of this view in 1912.

THE OLD WHIPPING POST AND STOCKS in 1903, still on view in the churchyard today.

CURTAIN ROAD, looking south from Old Street, with Rivington Street on the left, seen *c.* 1900. Curtain Road was very much a centre of the furniture-making trade. This had developed rapidly from the 1840s and by 1861 30 per cent of all London furniture makers worked in the East End. These included many Jewish firms and workers.

CURTAIN ROAD, looking north from Great Eastern Street in 1897. This picture is from George Newnes' *Round London*, which mentions the fire hazard caused by the concentration of the furniture trade in the area.

OLD STREET MAGISTRATES COURT, seen here *c.* 1908 when the building was two years old. The new court was not to the liking of the magistrates, who complained after a week of the noise from the adjacent North London Railway, the incessant buzz of a circular saw, the barking of captive dogs in the station yard, a gas engine safety valve and a steam hooter. It is to be hoped that any who came before the bench in June 1906 received a fair hearing.

THE CORNER OF COMMERCIAL ROAD AND SHOREDITCH HIGH STREET, looking south-west, showing the Unicorn public house. Antonio Bianchi, who made looking-glasses, moved out shortly after 1865, so this view dates before that time. The drinking fountain and street light both went when Great Eastern Street was cut through, directly behind where the photographer was standing, in 1876.

THE EAST SIDE OF SHOREDITCH HIGH STREET, looking north from the corner with French Place. Faith Brothers, on the corner at No. 148, traded there from 1900 to 1911 as hosiers, so this view is *c.* 1910.

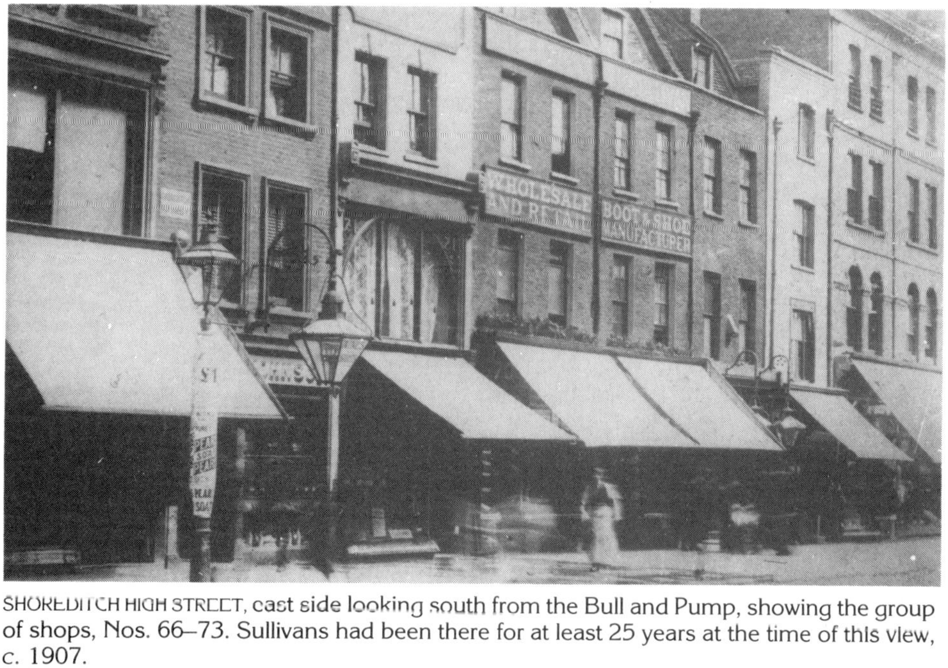


SHOREDITCH HIGH STREET, east side looking south from the Bull and Pump, showing the group of shops, Nos. 66–73. Sullivans had been there for at least 25 years at the time of this view, *c.* 1907.

HENRY DEARE'S FURNISHING SHOP, Nos. 307–11 Old Street; a photograph in a sale catalogue of 1895. At the time the business was being run by Alfred Beadman on lease and included upholstery workshops, showrooms and shop. It looks as though onlookers as well as staff have gathered for the view, an unusual inclusion in sale catalogues of the time.

CHARLES SQUARE and the Shoreditch Magistrates Court and Registrar's office *c.* 1900. Charles Square was a very good address in the early eighteenth century and survived intact until it was cleared for redevelopment in 1955–6. Only No. 16, the former courthouse, survived – in its later days it had been a health centre.

PHILIP BARNET AND HIS STAFF outside their workshop, No. 96 Curtain Road *c*. 1900. Next door is an upholsterers, the other dominant industry in the area.

WILLIAM HARPUR was a Shoreditch bookseller, who some time before 1856 had taken over an existing shop in City Road. In 1860 he moved to No. 32 Tabernacle Walk (later No. 58 Tabernacle Street) and these photographs, probably taken in the early 1890s, show the shop and the tiny garden squeezed in behind it. The site was cleared for demolition in 1895 and Harpur had a grand sale before moving to temporary premises at No. 36 across the road.

THE KINGSLAND CLUB CHAMBERS was a lodging house, one of many in Shoreditch at the time of this 1910 view. This one was at No. 277 Kingsland Road. In his *Life and Labour of the People of London* of 1902, Charles Booth notes the distinction between common lodging houses and those known 'by the more euphonious name of "chambers", and in those of a better class are to be found many young clerks and shop assistants who wish to husband their resources and . . . "cut a dash" in some other direction.' No. 277 was still used as a lodging house up to 1939 and may have been a victim of the Blitz in 1940.

HAGGERSTON LIBRARY, Nos. 234–236 Kingsland Road, seen here in the late 1890s. Shoreditch was slow to have its own public libraries and only did so after a public campaign in 1891. This was the first, opened in 1892 and extended a year later, the premises having been acquired from the Independant Gas Company with funding from Passmore Edwards. It closed in 1975 and after a long period of dereliction is to be converted to a night club.

THE BRITANNIA THEATRE, Hoxton Street, *c.* 1890. There were many theatres in nineteenth-century Shoreditch but the 'Brit' had the most faithful following. It had its origins in a saloon adjoining the Britannia Tavern in the early 1840s, founded by Sam Lane and managed after his death by his redoubtable wife Sarah until 1899. Built in 1858 a packed house could hold nearly 3,000 people for plays, music hall and pantomine. In use as a cinema after 1923, the 'Brit' was bombed in 1940 and demolished after the war.

THE DORSET WORKS YARD OF DOTTERIDGES, undertakers, on the east side of East Road in the 1870s. Dotteridges 'of London, Birmingham and Carrera' provided funeral hardware, furnishings, drapery, carriages and all extras for funerals. This view includes Samuel Dotteridge III and shows a courtyard that had formerly been part of a galleried inn. The firm later moved to offices on New North Road and moved from the area in 1985.

PITFIELD STREET, looking north from the junction with Old Street in 1896. The third building on the right, north of Boot Street, is the Variety Theatre, opened in 1870 and converted into a cinema after 1910. This is another view by George Newnes who was especially struck by the good meat that could be purchased at 2*d*. per pound and the apples at 6*d*. for a stone!

SHOREDITCH WORKHOUSE, later part of St Leonard's Hospital, Hoxton Street, *c.* 1910, showing the corner with the most inappropriately named Land of Promise. This building of 1863 replaced the earlier one of 1777, which had been served by James Parkinson, whose famous work on the palsy led to it being named after him. Edith Cavell was Assistant Matron from 1903 to 1906, after which she went to Belgium and in 1915 was executed by the Germans for helping British soldiers in her care to escape.

HOXTON STREET, east side, looking north towards Shoreditch Workhouse and including the Queen's Head public house, *c.* 1905.

HOXTON STREET, east side, showing the Admiral Keppel and Costers' Hall, *c.* 1910.

GREAT CAMBRIDGE STREET, looking north across the junction with Dunloe Street. Great Cambridge Street changed its name to Queensbridge Road in 1939. The block building on the right is St Saviour's Priory, an Anglican order founded by three St Margaret's sisters in Ash Grove, Hackney in 1866. There was a link with Haggerston from the earliest years, though the building in this view dates from 1887. The building fronting Queensbridge Road was replaced after 1976 and all other buildings in this view have gone.

EDWARD FENN'S LEATHER WAREHOUSE was at No. 22 Stoke Newington Church Street, throughout the 1890s. The proud owner and his shop front are seen here early in that decade.

## SECTION EIGHT

# Stoke Newington

AT THE BEGINNING OF THE NINETEENTH CENTURY Stoke Newington was largely rural, with settlement lines along Church Street, High Street and the Newington Green area. It was traversed by two watercourses, the Hackney Brook and the New River. The first significant development was in Albion Road by Thomas Cubitt in the early 1820s, and building gathered pace in the 1840s. But the real transformation took place in the years 1870 to 1914 when there was a four-fold increase in the number of buildings and overcrowding in some areas, though the area north of Lordship Park and Manor Road still consisted of larger houses. But the photographers' lenses were mainly occupied with High Street and Church Street, a preoccupation which is, to some extent reflected in this selection. The opening view looking east along Church Street is from a point just west of the gateway of St Mary's Old Church. Projecting forward on the right is the eighteenth-century Halstead House. This and the adjacent row were demolished in 1930 as part of operations to widen Albion Road. The Rose and Crown was relocated at the same time and the new building stands on the site of Halstead House. This view dates from the 1880s. (AB)

THE REAR OF FLEETWOOD HOUSE, which stood on the north side of Church Street, a little to the west of the present Fleetwood Street. This house was built *c.* 1634 by Sir Edward Hartopp, whose widow married the Cromwellian general, Charles Fleetwood. The Hartopp and Fleetwood families lived there until 1766. It was later a girls school, though by the date of this view, in the 1870s, the eastern part was divided into tenements for lodgers. It was demolished in 1872.

CHURCH STREET, looking east from Barn Street towards the Lordship Road and the Red Lion public house. From the left are the premises of Mr Johnson the gardener and the Vestry offices, Mrs Osborn's toyshop and, one house beyond, Edwin Porter the butcher, *c.* 1887. (AB)

ST MARY'S MISSION ROOMS AND DAY NURSERY, No. 106 Church Street. This had opened in 1885 offering a night school and boys' club and a venue for mothers' meetings with sales of clothes. It lasted until *c.* 1903, under the direction of Miss, later Sister, Annie Jefferson, *c.* 1887. (AB)

LOOKING WEST FROM ST MARY'S DAY NURSERY towards the Red Lion *c.* 1887. (AB)

THE RED LION and buildings to the west, *c*. 1887. The public house dates back to before 1697. The houses beyond included the Amethyst Club, opened in 1882 as coffee rooms and a working men's club, occupying No. 110 Church Street until 1917. The houses beyond the Red Lion were demolished in 1931. (AB)

CHURCH STREET by the junction with Albion Road, with a street sweeper leaning on his broom. This view of *c*. 1890 also shows the other side of Halstead House and the premises of John Stapleton, builder, at No. 197 Church Street.

NO. 124 CHURCH STREET, after it had ceased to be a toy shop, in 1895. This house also appears on p. 98. The house next door, No. 122, had formerly belonged to Pishey Thompson (d. 1862), author of a history of Boston.

CHURCH HOUSE AND CHURCH ROW, which formerly stood on the north side of Church Street, just east of St Mary's Old Church. Church Row was built in 1695 on the site of the manor house. Among many famous residents were John Howard, the prison reformer, and Frederick Mullet Evans (d. 1870) who owned *Punch*. In his time his house, No. 8, was visited by Dickens and Thackeray. The Row was demolished in 1932. Municipal offices are now on the site. *c.* 1887. (AB)

THIS, THE OLDEST EXTANT PHOTOGRAPH OF ANY HACKNEY SUBJECT, shows the Old Rectory in its last days, before demolition shortly after 1855. The rectory dated from at least the early sixteenth century and was timber framed with a tiled roof. The site is now occupied by St Mary's New Church.

ST MARY'S OLD CHURCH was almost completely rebuilt by William Patten, though the medieval nave and south porch remain. This view, *c.* 1890, shows the church after early-nineteenth-century restoration which gave the building a more Gothic appearance. Damaged by bombs in 1940, the church was again restored, but without its nineteenth-century north aisle. (AB)

PARADISE ROW 1882, a view looking north-east from Paradise Bridge. The western end of Stoke Newington Church Street has been completely transformed by the culverting of the New River after 1952 and rebuilding in the area. Paradise Row had been built from 1723 onwards and for more than a century housed bankers, brokers and manufacturers, but the LCC cleared all the houses in this view to build flats in 1936. (AB)

PARADISE ROW, from just east of Glebe Place looking west, in around 1890.

CLISSOLD PARK, the bandstand and the spire of the New Church, summer *c.* 1910. Originally a private estate, the park takes its names from the curate, Augustus Clissold who married into the Crawshay family, in the teeth of their opposition. After Clissold's death the estate was sold and after a public campaign acquired by the Metropolitan Board of Works as a park in 1889.

THE FORMER MANOR HOUSE BOARDING SCHOOL, on the north side of Church Street, to the east of Edwards Lane. This was opened in 1806 by Revd John Bransby. Edgar Allan Poe was a pupil there from 1817 to 1820. This view probably dates from 1880 when it was demolished.

THE WEST SIDE OF EDWARDS LANE, c. 1899, just before demolition to build the extension to the public library. The lane is named after Job Edwards, who built much of Church Row and who lived in a house on the corner of Church Street and Edwards Lane.

THE CORNER OF LORDSHIP AND MANOR ROADS, c. 1874. The house with the private road notice (issued by the Manor of Stoke Newington and still run by trustees of the Eade family at this date) was to become the site of Manor Road Presbyterian Church from 1884 to 1971.

BEFORE THE ADVENT OF TARMAC, roads were much dustier than they are now and, accordingly, local authorities had to make efforts to keep the dust down. This magnificent machine was one of Stoke Newington's water carts, about to leap into action one summer *c.* 1910.

BOATING POOLS were not always easy to accommodate in the grounds of suburban houses, but the Allen family managed it in a dog-leg of their garden at No. 186 Lordship Road. The pool is about twice the length of the boat, though the railings are a safety feature rather than the limit of the garden, which extended to Andrews Road. From a slide of 1905.

THE NORTH SIDE OF NEWINGTON GREEN and the Unitarian Chapel, a view of c. 1855. The chapel was built by Presbyterians in 1708 but became Unitarian at the end of the eighteenth century. This view was taken before the building works of 1860 which gave it a new stucco front. The building to the left was replaced by a bank and those to the right became R.A. Enright's estate agents in 1896.

THE PUMPING STATION, Green Lane, a view looking north *c.* 1860. This had been built in 1852 to the design of the company's engineer, William Chadwell Mylne, in conjunction with the filter beds on the other side of the road. The original steam engines were removed in 1936 and the building used only for storage from 1946 onwards. With the advent of the new ring water main round London, the whole future of the filter beds and the reservoirs is under threat at the time of writing.

JACKSON'S TEA GARDENS, which stood on the north side of Seven Sisters Road, opposite the junction with Blackstock Road. A view dating from *c.* 1860. Robert Jackson was still listed there in a directory of 1860, but the house and gardens probably went shortly afterwards, as part of the changes that followed on from the opening of Finsbury Park in 1869.

ST MARY'S NEW CHURCH AND PARK CRESCENT, 1875. The building to the left is the lodge of Clissold House. St Mary's New Church, built in 1855 to a design by George Gilbert Scott, did not have the spire added to its tower until 1890. Park Crescent was renumbered as part of Stoke Newington Church Street in 1937. The lodge had gone by 1894.

NOS. 157–61 STOKE NEWINGTON HIGH STREET in 1883. The floor of Love's shop was below street level and there was a step down immediately inside the door. A branch of Barclay's Bank now occupies this site.

THIS AND THE NEXT PAGE show a panoramic view of the funeral cortège of General William Booth arriving outside the gates of Abney Park Cemetery, Stoke Newington High Street, 29 August 1912. The bend in the road is a trick of the camera, which has panned round to take in the whole view: the massed ranks of the Salvation Army, the crowds of spectators, even fellow photographers on the roof of Whitford the undertakers. Abney Park was founded in 1839 from the grounds of the Abney House estate and succeeded Bunhill Fields as a principal nonconformist cemetery in North London, though it also served as a public cemetery for the whole of north-east London. Initially, careful attention was given to the planting, but as the economics of cemetery management changed, this pattern was spoiled by ever denser burials. Abney Park Cemetery remained a public company until 1978, when the cemetery was sold to Hackney Council for £1. Restoration work and conservation schemes are now in progress, though care is being taken to preserve some of the wilder

areas of the grounds which provide perfect habitats for many species of birds and animals. Not only were the headquarters of the Salvation Army in Hackney for many years, but the Booths also had a long association with the area. The General himself moved to No. 1 Cambridge Villas (now part of the site of St Joseph's Hospice) in 1865. A year later he moved to Gore Road and in 1880 to No. 114 Clapton Common. The family's last address in Hackney was Rockwood Road. The local journalist, J.R. Spratling, editor of the *North London Guardian*, was a witness to the funeral procession:

During the early morning rain fell in torrents, but its effect upon the size of the crowd was scarcely perceptible. The great procession of between 5,000 and 6,000 Salvationists which was marshalled on the Embankment, left the headquarters at 11.30. A flag was placed at the

head and foot of the coffin, upon which were laid the General's hat and bible. The breast plate was uncovered. At the side of the hearse, almost obscuring the wheels was a device in green, upon which, in white letters were printed the words 'He laid down his sword'. A shield of green bore the inscription in white 'William Booth, founder and General of the Salvation Army, born 10 April 1829, died 20 August 1912. Born again of the Spirit 1845. Birth of the Salvation Army, 1865.' Immediately preceding the hearse was a brougham filled with beautiful wreaths, among which were those from the King and the German Emperor . . .

Every City thoroughfare was thronged and the route thence, which lay through Shoreditch, Kingsland and Stoke Newington. What may be termed the last stage in the striking procession stretched from Dalston Junction along High Street, Stoke Newington to the cemetery, a distance of about a mile, and here great crowds pressed in from the numerous side streets intent on catching a glimpse of the impressive scene. By noon the footways were lined with sympathisers, but soon after one o'clock, when thousands more were able to join the throng owing to the business half holiday in the district, the people were massed ten deep. At the windows of the shops and houses anxious spectators were

gathered and on the roofs of buildings many groups of men and boys huddled in expectant attitudes . . .

For two hours the multitude had stood calmly awaiting the funeral cortege and spent the time in subdued conversation. Then when the strains of the leading band was heard there was a sudden hush, men doffed their caps and the earnest faces of the spectators remained fixed on the passing spectacle. Long and slow as the march from the city had been the women soldiers evinced no sign of fatigue. At ten to three the head of the inspiring procession reached the cemetery and half an hour later there arrived the bier bearing the coffin . . . by half past three the last contingent wheeled in through the gates and the final stage of a most memorable procession through the streets of London was completed.

THE INVALID ASYLUM, No. 187 Stoke Newington High Street, in the late 1890s. The Home Hospital for Women was founded in 1825 by Mary Lister, aunt of the famous surgeon, and it moved to No. 187 in 1830. It took up to 26 patients at a time from all over London until its closure in 1939. No. 187 itself was built in 1712. The house is now council offices.

NOS 144 TO 154 STOKE NEWINGTON HIGH STREET, seen here *c.* 1872. Behind the gates was the North London Brewery Tap. Woolworths now occupy the site of Volckman and Mason's shops.

SECTION NINE

# Upper Clapton and Stamford Hill

THE NAME 'CLAPTON' – originally Clopton – is Anglo-Saxon, meaning 'the farm on the hill'. This would have been the highest point of the area, probably the ridge above the Lea where Springfield Park now stands. Both Upper Clapton, which I have taken here as broadly that area north of the Lea Bridge Road, and Stamford Hill kept their open spaces and large houses longer than other areas of the borough and Springfield Park was the last major open space in the area when it was saved as a public park in 1905. This section looks at the streets, houses and shops of an area that before the First World War remained very much a retreat from the bustle of inner London. The first view shows the Swan Hotel, Clapton Common and the Clapton–Moorgate horse tram in the summer of 1880. The service had been opened up five years before in July 1875 by the North Metropolitan Tramways company. (AB)

THIS THATCHED COTTAGE stood at the west end of Spring Hill, adjoining a private road that ran to Buccleuch Cottages, and is seen here in 1880. Probably built on common land in the late eighteenth century, it remained occupied until *c*. 1917. After a period being empty it was burnt out in 1919. The building is on a slope, so it is bigger than this photograph, taken north, would suggest. (AB)

THE WEST SIDE OF UPPER CLAPTON showing Nos. 109 to 115. Brown's the florist was quite new at the time of this view, which is *c*. 1889, though discrepancies between shops listed in the directories and those shown on the view make it hard to date. (AB)

CLAPTON COMMON POND AND BUCCLEUCH TERRACE, from a postcard taken at the turn of the century. Buccleuch Terrace, built *c.* 1825, was demolished by Hackney Council *c.* 1952 to build the present block of flats that stands on the site.

CEDAR HOUSE, Stamford Hill, showing the front lawn and drive. This stood at the south side of the end of Upper Clapton Road at the junction with Stamford Hill, was built *c.* 1750–60 and took its name from a cedar tree in the grounds. For many years the owner was Dr Charles Aveling, but after his death in 1903 the house remained empty until it was demolished in 1908. Shops and flats now occupy the site. A view of *c.* 1900.

NOS. 11–21 UPPER CLAPTON ROAD, *c.* 1895. Hugh Thomas' main premises were on Stoke Newington Church Street and his yards are rather grandly titled 'Upper Clapton Depository' on the sign over the door. Further on, at the end of the row, can be seen the wall of Brooke House. These houses were all badly damaged in the same raid in October 1940 that hit Brooke House, and were demolished after the war. (JC)

ELECTRIFICATION OF HORSE TRAMWAYS was begun in London in 1898 and by 1903 was in full swing. Because the LCC was opposed to overhead wiring a conduit system was introduced with collection of electricity from the track. This is the east side of Stamford Hill, near the Bird Cage Tavern, *c.* 1906 with work in progress for the conversion which reopened on 4 February 1907. The conduit, which was not a success, had to be renewed again after 1918.

IMPROVING THE IMAGE OF THE FAMILY BUSINESS turn-of-the-century style. William Smallshaw started his second-hand furniture shop at No. 240 Stoke Newington High Street in 1864. He moved to Willow Place (later No. 10 Stamford Hill) in 1873. By 1904 his son had refronted the shop and moved up-market into antiques. Perhaps the local phenomenon of gentrification has its earlier precursors . . .

THE JUNCTION with Lea Bridge Road and Upper Clapton Road as it appeared *c.* 1870. The shops in the area in the 1872 directory were a hairdresser, grocer and bootmaker. The building in the distance was in use as one of Hackney's many private schools. The lamp standard adjoined the drinking fountain that can be seen on p. 46. The row would appear to have been demolished *c.* 1880 and replaced by the shops seen on p. 122.

VINE AND MYRTLE COTTAGES and Snewin's premises stood on the west side of Upper Clapton Road, just to the south of Clapton Railway station. Vine Cottage, much altered, still survives; the other buildings were demolished shortly after the construction of Gunton Road in 1889. Photograph 1886. (AB)

BROOKE HOUSE, a view from Upper Clapton Road and the corner of Kenninghall Road looking north *c.* 1910 and a view of part of the south range with staff and possibly patients *c.* 1900. Brooke House, which had it origins in a late-fifteenth-century house, was much enlarged in the mid-sixteenth century and owes the appearance of its street elevation to the end of the eighteenth century. It took its name from Sir Fulke Greville, the poet and dramatist who was created Baron Brooke in 1621, but from 1758 it was used as a private lunatic asylum. Bombed in October 1940 and again in 1944, the remains were demolished in 1954–5. A school stands on the site.

THE ROW OF HOUSES on the west side of Upper Clapton Road that replaced the buildings seen in the photo on p. 120, seen here in the summer of 1904. The horse tram service had been extended from its terminus at the White Swan, an old coaching stop, right through to Stamford Hill only four years before. The service had originally been run by the North Metropolitan Tramways Company; which was taken over by the LCC in 1896 and electrified in 1909.

SPRINGFIELD COTTAGE stood on the north side of Springfield at the bottom of the slope and near the junction with Big Hill. The original cottage had been steadily added to and it had a fine view out over the Lea. The antiquarian Florence Bagust visited it in 1908 to take this photograph, when it had been empty for some years; shortly afterwards it was demolished for the construction of Hawkwood Mount.

THE OLD FOUNTAIN, SPRING HILL. A view looking east with the entrance to Springfield Park on the right, *c.* 1910. The grounds of Springfield had been acquired as a public park only five years before.

THE RIVER LEA AND THE MARSHES, a photograph taken from an upper window at the back of Stainforth House by N. Hanbury, a relative of Frederick Hanbury, the owner. The gardens and the pleasant view have now gone, covered by the houses and back gardens of Craven Walk, and Ashtead and Lingwood Roads, but Stainforth House, built in the early nineteenth century, still stands. 1906.

FLOODING was a perennial problem in the Lea Valley as these two views show. The top one, near Lea Bridge, may have been taken during the inundation of May 1889; the lower is a winter view looking south at the Robin Hood public house. The ferry looks ready to brave the enlarged Lea; in calmer weather it took passengers across to Walthamstow Marshes and was still marked in the Ordnance Survey maps in 1954. Annual reports of Hackney's Surveyor and Medical Officer of Health ultimately resulted in clearance of many of the riverside houses along the Lea.

SECTION TEN

# The River Lea

THIS IDYLLIC SCENE of the Robin Hood public house and adjoining houses introduces Hackney's eastern boundary, the River Lea, also a navigation route and a source of drinking water. The first improvements in the river were made in Elizabethan times and prior to 1767 a water-wheel and small works were constructed at Lea Bridge, owned by the Hackney Waterworks. Increases in trade and population prompted later improvements in the navigation, including an additional channel in 1833–4 and waterworks at Lea Bridge in 1829, where the East London Waterworks Company built filter beds. But the state of the water was causing concern by the time of this photograph, in the late 1860s, as Walthamstow and Leyton poured untreated sewage into the river. The problem of water – too much, too little in drought years, or too unhealthy – was to continue until improved reservoirs were constructed further north from 1910 onwards. (GJ)

HORSE SHOE POINT was once joined to the west bank of the Lea. This 1888 view was taken just to the south of the bend, looking north from a path leading to Spring Lane. In the middle distance is Willowfield Cottage, which featured in many early-nineteenth-century views of the Lea. By 1894 the course of the Lea had altered to make the point an island and Horse Shoe Bridge was built level with the cottage. Willowfield Cottage was demolished somewhere between 1901 and 1915. (AB)

THE SECOND LEA BRIDGE, built in 1820, seen here from the north, *c.* 1890. This replaced the first wooden bridge of 1757 and was rebuilt shortly after this view in 1892. To the left is the timber yard of Essex Wharf and above the bridge is the original Prince of Wales Hotel.

SUMMER DAYS AT THE ROBIN HOOD, then as now a popular visiting place, seen here in 1896 (top) and 1890. The ferry boat is visible in both views and the flags may well be out for a local regatta. Lemonade and ginger beer are being served from the stall. Subject to constant flooding, all the houses were cleared before 1915, though the white building in the centre, the Beehive, was rebuilt. (AB)

THE WHITE HOUSE, Hackney Marshes, taken by the Leyton photographer Alfred Wire in 1911. Noted on Rocque's map of 1745 at Tyler's Ferry, The White House stood on a bend on the east side of the Lea in Hackney Marshes and had it own fishery, until pollution killed the fish. For many years it was owned by the Beresford family, whose name is associated with the place and who sold it in 1897. In 1911 the LCC refused to renew the licence, due to problems of late drinking, and although it was up for sale it did not find a buyer. It was demolished sometime after 1913.

THE WHITE HART, Temple Mills, stood right on the boundary with Leyton on the west side of the Waterworks river, and adjoined the old mill. The antiquarian Benjamin Clarke visited the site in the early 1890s and noted that the mill machinery had already been removed. The building in this view was rebuilt in the twentieth century.

BARGES avoided the meandering sections of the Lea north of Temple Mills by using the Hackney Cut Navigation. This view of *c.* 1900 shows the small bridge from Millfields, just south of the Prince of Wales public house.

TO CATER FOR PLEASURE-BOATING there were punts and skiffs for hire on the Lea. This view shows the Jolly Angler's public house, Middlesex Wharf, in 1884. To the fore are the men and boats of F.H. Fullcher, behind are Hammond's Cottages and the yard of Vincent Green, boat builder. This area of Middlesex Wharf was cleared in the 1930s as a health measure due to frequent flooding, though no doubt the boats and beer of the Jolly Anglers would still be popular today. (AB)

THE EFFECTS OF THE FLOOD of May 1903 were not confined to horse trams (p. 47). These adventurous small boys with their raft are sailing past the back of the cottages on Middlesex Wharf over the inundated North Millfields.

A VIEW DOWN LITTLE HILL *c.* 1900, looking towards the Lea and the Robin Hood public house, with the Gospel Ferry Mission Hall on the left. A contemporary writer described this as an 'interesting hamlet of picturesque cottages and narrow lanes' but it was all swept away in the 1930s to build the present blocks of flats on the site.

VERNON'S BOAT HOUSE, Spring Hill, seen here in 1905. In 1881 the River Lea Amateur Rowing Association was established to organize competitions on the Lea. These boat houses at the foot of Spring Hill were the base for many local rowing clubs.

SPECTATORS AT THE LEA REGATTA, 1895. The event was then 30 years old and by the 1870s 12 clubs competed. This view was also taken near the bottom of Spring Hill.

A LONDON AND GENERAL HORSE BUS resting at the Stamford Hill end of its route to Elephant and Castle, which ran via Clapton, Dalston Junction and Shoreditch, *c.* 1902.

RECTORY ROAD STATION looking north along the down platform, with a Liverpool Street train pulling in. The station was opened by the Great Eastern Railway in 1872; this view can be dated to 1906 from the newspaper boards which announce the fall of Port Arthur to the Japanese in the war with Russia in that year. The locomotive is probably a Holden 2-4-2 tank. A Charles Martin postcard.

SECTION ELEVEN

# Out and About

THE MIDDLE OF THE NINETEENTH CENTURY saw considerable improvements to help people get about in the Hackney area. Horse bus services began in the 1830s, improving on the frequency of the previous coaches into the City of London, and these were followed by horse tramways in the 1870s. The first railway in the area was the North London line, opened in 1850 and cutting a swathe through the centre of Hackney, followed by the main line into Liverpool Street in the late 1860s and the North London extension to Broad Street opened in 1865, which did equal damage to Shoreditch. Stoke Newington got its rail connection in 1872. For the more independent there was the new craze for bicycles in the later years of the century, as well as horse brake outings and, for the better-off, early motor cars. This section looks at the means of getting about and some of the more select delights for those who stayed at home. The view on this page shows an LCC horse tram on Graham Road, probably taken shortly before the route was electrified in 1913.

BROAD STREET STATION FRONT, seen here *c.* 1900. The imposing terminus of the North London Railway was built in 1865 as the NLR's City extension. Although the frontage is in the City, much of the eastern side of the station lay in Shoreditch and the arches used for the new line cut through the site of the medieval priory of Holy Trinity. Broad Street station was sadly swept away in 1985–6 for the construction of the Broadgate development.

SHOREDITCH STATION was the North London's station at the corner of Old Street and Kingsland Road, and opened in 1865. This view shows the original building, which was rebuilt by the LMS in 1927. The new station was bomb-damaged and closed in 1941, but is still in use as commercial premises. A view of *c.* 1900.

THE ORIGINAL TERMINUS of the Eastern Counties Railway (later the Great Eastern) fronted onto Shoreditch High Street. Built in 1840, it remained the main GER terminus until replaced by Liverpool Street station in 1874. Rebuilt as a goods station in 1881 it was burned out in 1964 and much of the site is now an NCP car park. This view dates from c. 1860.

RAIL SERVICES allowed East Enders to escape from their crowded streets and courts. Holidays were beyond the reach of many, but a working substitute was summer hop-picking in Kent. This view shows the Harrison family of Hoxton pausing for a photograph at Horsmonden(?) in 1906.

THE COPPING FAMILY just about to set out for a spin to Epping Forest in their Model T Ford, c. 1914. The construction of the rail link to Chingford in the early 1870s made this a popular destination for East Londoners.

THE MADISON FAMILY AND FRIENDS with pony and trap in 1906. Thomas Madison had a glass business in Craven Street, Hoxton.

THE BICYCLE MADE FOR TWO is in the capable hands of Joseph Wilbeforce and Mrs Getrude Richardson, respectively organizer and worker at the Orchard Mission in Well Street. This was run by Cambridge Heath Congregational Church. The location of this view is not recorded, but may well have been Epping Forest and was taken in 1919.

THE STOKE NEWINGTON CYCLING CLUB gathered outside their headquarters at the Swan public house, Upper Clapton, in either 1886 or 1887.

AN ALL-WOMAN'S OUTING BY HORSEBRAKE, captured by F. Poulter possibly at High Beech in the summer of 1909. The stone jugs, with lemonade or ginger beer, suggests that this might have been a temperance outing, and the address of the photographer, Holcroft Road, South Hackney, may indicate a trip organized by one of the local missions, possibly the Orchard Street Mission.

NEARER TO HOME was the St Philip's Church, Dalston, infants' treat of 1912. The church closed in 1953 when the parish was united with that of Holy Trinity, and the premises on Richmond Road were later demolished.

SOUTHEND was a popular destination for Hackney people, but the London Tilbury and Southend Railway did not usually go to the trouble of decorating its engines in this fashion! This is the front end of LTSR 4-4-2 tank *Thundersley* at Plaistow shed, on the occasion of George V's coronation in 1911.

A GOOD LOCAL DAY OUT was always to be had in Victoria Park, which was taken over by East Enders in 1846 – there was no formal opening. A special feature was the Chinese pagoda which stood on the larger island in the boating lake and is glimpsed in the early 1880s, top view, above the trees. It had been acquired in 1847, having formerly served as the entrance to the Chinese Collection at Hyde Park Corner. Demolished after the Second World War, it is now scheduled to be replaced by a modern copy. Below is a view of another popular feature, the Aviary, taken *c.* 1905, which had been in existence at least ten years previously.

THE BOATING LAKE, Victoria Park, one high summer at the turn of the century.

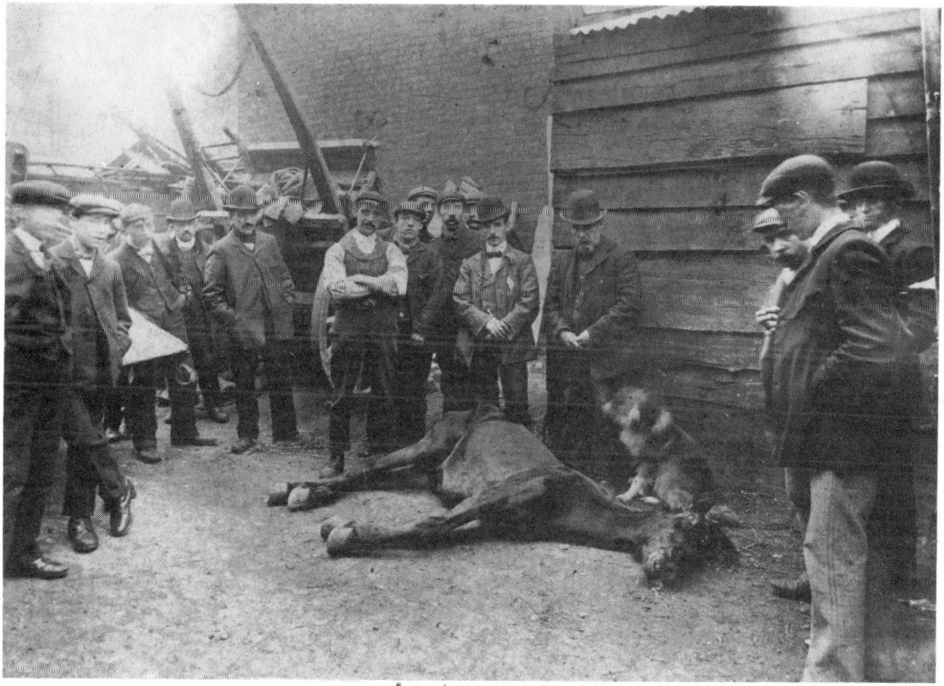
NOT ABOUT TO GO ANYWHERE; a group of traders round a dead horse in Russia Lane, Bethnal Green, 1907.

SOMETHING OF A HACKNEY INSTITUTION in his lifetime was Frederick Peters, 'Blind Fred'. Born blind in 1871 he sold matches from the same spot in Hackney churchyard for over 40 years until his death in 1933. The place is marked by a memorial plaque with the words, 'Hereby was seen for many years Blind Fred, a sunny soul' and below in Braille, 'One thing I know, that whereas I was blind, now I see.' (John 9, 25.)

SECTION TWELVE

# The Poor, the Sick, and the Damned

TO MINISTER TO THE NEEDS of the poor and the sick occupied many institutions and individuals in the period covered by this book. The poor lived in dread of the union workhouses, established in 1836 and not abolished until 1930. Shoreditch's workhouse later became St Leonard's Hospital. Hackney's – which also covered Stoke Newington – replaced the earlier parish workhouse at the eastern end of Homerton High Street and became Hackney Hospital. In both cases the change of function grew out of earlier infirmary facilities provided by the unions. Other hospitals had their origins directly from medical need, like the Children's Hospital on Hackney Road or to serve specific communities, like the German Hospital. Charitable initiatives and institutions were legion, and other sections have included almshouses. Here it has only been possible to look at two unusual examples. Finally, in all poor areas missions were at work trying to save souls, all too often working in back streets away from the camera. This page shows an omnibus pram in the grounds of Hackney Workhouse in 1902.

THE SCENE IS CLAPTON BATHS on 4 January 1911, when the Mayor of Hackney, W. Fenton Jones, presided over a dinner for 'the necessitious poor of Hackney'. The Distress Committee provided roast beef, roast mutton, greens and potatoes for the first course, followed by plum pudding and accompanied by mineral water and coffee. The local paper reported, 'The Mayor and Mayoress attended in state, accompanied by several of their children and after the repast the Mayor went round the tables and thoughtfully handed to the men packages of tobacco and pipes; the Mayoress to the women and children, sweets etc, also dolls dressed by [her] daughters and useful presents of books. An instantaneous flash light photograph of the assembly was taken by Reginald Cleare of Lower Clapton Road. The report of the flashlight was so loud that many in the huge hall thought some of the Houndsditch anarchists had got into the building, but their fears were soon allayed.'

BY CONTRAST here are members of the Stoke Newington Tradesmen's Association doing themselves proud at their ninth annual banquet at the Liverpool Street Hotel on 1 March 1906. Besides the Tradesmen's Association, Stoke Newington councillors were also fond of their annual dinners – paid for at their own expense, not the ratepayers' – and numerous photographs exist of these occasions. Distortion on the wide-angle lenses used sometimes produced some rather lugubrious expressions, as if the participants had eaten well, but not wisely.

A NEW YEAR CELEBRATION at the Children's Hospital, Hackney Road, *c.* 1900.

THE CITY MISSION maintained an Ayah's Home at No. 26 King Edward's Road from the turn of the century, which later moved to No. 4 and closed in 1941. According to Alec Roberts, who included it in his article in *Living London* Vol. III of 1906, it was 'a great boon to the Indian women who come and go between here and India as nurses or attendants on ladies or their children'; in all probability it was also very convenient for those ladies who did not have to maintain native servants at their own expense while in England.

THE GERMAN HOSPITAL had been established on Dalston Lane in 1845 to serve a strong local German community and moved to new purpose-built premises to the east of Fassett Square in 1865. The hospital continued to be staffed by Germans until the Second World War when all the staff were interned. The hospital had always offered its services to all local people, whether they were of German origin or not, and after 40 years under the NHS it has recently closed. The top view shows the Ritson Road entrance in June 1906, possibly when a garden party was in progress, the lower a corner of the children's ward at about the same date.

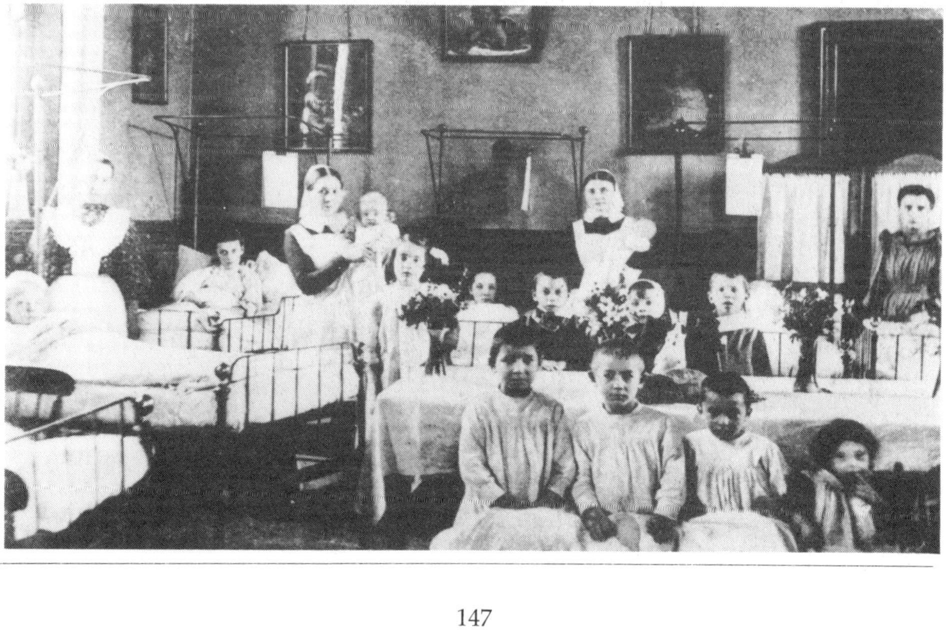

MISSION HALLS of various denominations, or none at all, were a common phenomenon in Hackney and Shoreditch; often poorly documented they can be very hard to trace. A particularly obscure one was the Stonebridge Common Gospel Mission, whose tiny hall adjoined Stonebridge Common, in an as yet unlocated back street, where the donkey is resting from his labours for the Lord, *c.* 1900.

SECTION THIRTEEN

# Schooldays

THE LONDON SCHOOL BOARD was formed in 1870, the ancestor of the Inner London Education Authority. Prior to that date the majority of education had been provided by private schools or by bodies supervised by religious bodies. Hackney had been famous for its many private schools, but by 1914 the balance had shifted decidedly to the state sector. This section covers both private and public provision, beginning with Berger Road Girls' School celebrating Empire Day in May 1909.

TWO LONG-STANDING RIVALS IN HACKNEY were the Hackney Church of England Grammar School, Clarence Road (above), and the Hackney Proprietary Grammar School, both founded in 1830. The latter was barred to the children of shop-owners in Hackney. Indignant parents then formed the Church of England School, according to one early pupil, Benjamin Clarke, who described a schoolboy battle when the two schools joined forces against the Free and Parochial children in Hackney churchyard. The two schools amalgamated before 1848 on the Clarence Road site and the Sutton Place premises became Sutton Lodge, a private house. The Clarence Road school closed in 1895 and after four years as a mineral drinks factory was sold and demolished *c.* 1909. Sutton Lodge survived the clearance of the neighbouring houses for the Metal Box Factory, but was demolished for extensions before 1960. Both views *c.* 1886. (AB)

STAMFORD HILL AND CLAPTON SCHOOL FOR GIRLS, No. 96 Stamford Hill, on the corner with Lynmouth Road, seen here *c.* 1906 before it moved to No. 118. Kept by the Misses Henderson and Rothery it was typical of the many small private schools that once flourished in the area.

PARADISE HOUSE in Stoke Newington Church Street was home to a boarding school for boys from 1879 to 1919. This view of 1913 shows a gym lesson. The school magazine reveals that, among other activities, the programme of the Essay Society for 1912–13 included recitations, a debate on the theme 'that it is never justifiable to kill animals for pleasure' (motion won) and a 'vivid lantern lecture on the Boer War'.

THE PROBLEM OF EDUCATING WORKHOUSE CHILDREN existed before the formation of the unions in 1836 – workhouses were usually unsatisfactory. Shoreditch attempted to solve the problem by building a school out at Brentwood in 1854; enlarged in 1870 it was jointly managed for Shoreditch and Hackney until 1885, and for Hackney alone thereafter, and could cater for up to 550 children. This is the front *c.* 1898.

THE INTERIOR OF THE WOODWORKING SHOP AT BRENTWOOD about the same year. The school also accommodated half-timers. Four years earlier the school had been at the centre of a scandal when nurse Elizabeth Gillespie, a cruel disciplinarian, pushed a girl downstairs and killed her. The ensuing enquiry uncovered an atmosphere of violence and poor management and many staff were dismissed.

THE SCHOOL TOOK A KEEN INTEREST IN OUTDOOR GAMES and there was an annual athletic sports day. These two views were taken by W. Selfe on the 1898 day. The large gentleman may be one of the governors – he does not seem to be rushing to help with the wheelbarrow race.

SPORT AND EXERCISE became more important for schools in the 1890s – and not just for boys. This is the Morning Lane School Swedish Drill class taken at some time at the turn of the century.

A JUNIOR CLASS AT GAYHURST ROAD SCHOOL about to draw flowers. Between the years 1907 and 1913.

GAYHURST ROAD SCHOOL INFANTS proudly displaying art work, also from the period 1907–13.

VISUAL AIDS CAME EARLY TO SCHOOLS; a lantern slide lecture given at Stoke Newington Grammar School *c.* 1900. The school, founded in 1886 to provide a commercially-based education, was sited at Nos. 6–8 Manor Road and closed in 1925. The prospectus, from which this view was taken, emphasizes that lantern lectures were given only in the winter – presumably boys were expected to be outside more in the warmer months.

THE BUTTERS CHILDREN in the back garden of 'Parkfield', No. 49 King Edward Road, *c.* 1875. Their father, Walter Butters, was a local builder who had ensured that his own house had a larger garden than its neighbours. The elaborate walks show up in the Ordnance Survey map of 1870. The fussy ornamental garden is typical of the time.

MR SPENCER'S HOUSE AND GARDEN at Woodberry Down, seen from the adjacent field *c.* 1865. The house, earlier known as Cintra Cottage, was probably built at the turn of the nineteenth century, when the fashion for gothic cottages was at its height. A previous resident was A.J. Freire Marreco, whose friend Francisco de Paula Sant-lago, dedicated a set of quadrilles, named after localities, whose title page included a view of the cottage.

SECTION FOURTEEN

# Home and Garden

DOMESTIC VIEWS provide the most intimate glimpses of people's lives – and before 1914 are comparatively rare. Many areas of Hackney remained green up to the First World War, with many prosperous houses, and this selection includes views of one house whose owner commissioned a commercial survey. Back gardens were important for the less well-off – the Sunday flower market in Columbia Road had a long tradition and people queued for surplus plants given away from Victoria Park at certain times of the year. This wedding group has done well for flowers – the photograph was found in No. 10 Kenmure Road and could have been taken in the back garden there c. 1910.

THE FRONT ELEVATION AND LIVING ROOM of No. 183 Lower Clapton Road, taken *c.* 1910. For almost a hundred years the house was owned by the Gaviller family, who commissioned a fine album of black and white views and some autochromes, which form the earliest colour photographic views of any Hackney subject. The house was used by the Salvation Army after 1912 and was gutted by fire in 1927. The remains were demolished in 1933 as part of the clearances for the ugly and ill-fated Powell House council estate.

EITHER WILLIAM OR AUGUSTINE in the garden of No. 183, almost overshadowed by the giant hogweed (top). It was from gardens like the Gaviller's that the hogweed escaped to become a menace along the banks of the River Lea. Below is a print taken from one of the autochromes showing one of the walks and the back view of the house.

AN ECHO OF THE BUTTER'S GARDEN, this is the Smith's back garden with members of the family, No. 119 Rendlesham Road, Clapton *c.* 1914.

# ACKNOWLEDGEMENTS

All the photographs in this book have been taken from prints held by the London Borough of Hackney's Archives Department. The Department has been able to copy many originals held by other institutions, businesses and private individuals and the author and the publishers would like to thank the following for allowing their photographs to be used in this book:

Associated Financial Services Ltd (p. 93b) • Mrs Rosalind Bradley and Mr S. Barnett (p. 89) • Bush Boake Allen Ltd (p. 2) • Mr Coppin (pp. 48, 136t) Crown Berger Europe Ltd (pp. 64t and b) • Mr J. Dowding (pp. 72b, 73) Mrs Edna Edwards and Isobel Watson (pp. 70–71) • Mr N.W. Gibbs (p. 137t) Greater London Record Office & History Library (p. 30) • *Hackney Gazette* (p. 82) • Mr Ted Harrison (pp. 135b) • Mr L.G.E. Keen (p. 46) • Mr Tom King (p. 141b) • London Borough of Waltham Forest, Vestry House Museum (p. 128t) • Mr A. Newton (pp. 154b, 155t) • Mrs Mary Poulton (p. 136b) Mr John Rayment (p. 156b) • Royal Commission for Historic Monuments (p. 92b) • Mr John Smallshaw (p. 119t and b, 137b).

The author would also like to thank Godfrey New Photographics, Jenny Golden and John Newman.